PERFECT PITCHING FOR EXECUTIVES IN THE HIDDEN JOB MARKET

The Insider's Strategy for Winning in C-Suite
Job Interviews for $250K to $1 Million Jobs

PERFECT PITCHING FOR EXECUTIVES IN THE HIDDEN JOB MARKET

The Insider's Strategy for Winning in C-Suite
Job Interviews for $250K to $1 Million Jobs

Rainer Maria Morita

ISBN: 978-1-915147-22-6 (Paperback)

Library of Congress Cataloging-in-Publication Data:

1. Job interviewing 2. Job hunting 3. Job hunting and Career Guides Perfect Pitching for Executives in the Hidden Job Market Authored by Rainer Maria Morita

LCCN:

With your perfect pitch,
towards your next perfect hidden job.

CONTENTS

INTRODUCTION

Is your pitch perfect? Most executives would respond "No," or perhaps even ask: What exactly do you mean by a "pitch?"

The truth is that, while corporate leaders know and use pitching concepts to sell their brands all the time, they often fail to use these concepts when selling themselves. This problem is even more obvious when we look at hiring and interview scenarios in the elusive Hidden Job Market, where a clearly spelled-out job description is often missing, and lack of clarity governs the beginning of the conversation. Since I have already created my own method for navigating the Hidden Job Market called the Morita Method, I have decided to write a book focusing on perfect interview pitching in the Hidden Job Market as well.

Although I have described the Morita Method in other books, the core of what makes my method successful in Hidden Job Market interviews is that it allows you to make the best and most convincing pitch for you as the right candidate for the job. This is what I refer to as Perfect Pitching - creating the ideal conditions for your pitch to be successful. My clients are executives earning in the range of $200 thousand to $1 million; this book is therefore aimed at these executives and executive contenders in any Industry, Including private equity and venture capital.

Pitching successfully during your interview is a bit like having a perfect executive *résumé*: no one cares who prepared your *résumé*, as long as it's impeccable. In other words, you don't need to become a master at executive *résumé* writing: instead, you can outsource this to a pro. In the same way, you don't need to master the pitching process on your own, but can rely on the aid of a pitching expert who can guide you through this process.

Although nothing can fully replace a real-life "pitch doctor," my goal in this book is to provide you with some of the advantages and insights to honing your pitch that can come from working directly with a pitching expert.

If you are an executive reading this book, you have likely spent many hours honing your craft and getting to where you are. Congratulations! No doubt a good deal of your success has come from your ability to pitch successfully, at least in the right moments. If you are reading this book, however, you also realize that to go above and beyond, you cannot be an occasionally good pitcher of ideas; you must be the best pitcher around, period. And perhaps more importantly, you need to do this consistently!

The ability to pitch consistently and excellently is tied to one thing that may surprise you: *you must be able to tell a story.* Crafting a narrative that ropes in the interviewer and prepares them to receive your value offer - and thus to accept that value offer when it is made - is at the heart of what I call Perfect Pitching.

The beauty of Perfect Pitching is that it applies to all interview situations - from internal cases such as promotion or secondments to external cases like job searches with headhunters or corporate decision-makers. These techniques are also extremely effective for networking interviews, in which your goal is to have the opposite side introduce you to a decision-maker and help you to secure an interview. It also applies to other business pitching scenarios, in which you have a short time frame to convince someone to take action.

The interview scenario that this book is most directly aimed at, as mentioned above, is that of *hidden* job interviews - in other words, interviews for positions that are filled before they get publicly advertised. Don't forget, however - any networking opportunity can quickly turn into a hidden job market interview if you play your cards right and tell your story in a compelling way. The fast track towards a high-paying executive position lies in the Hidden Job Market, and in the ability to create, rather than find, your perfect job.

Many business decisions are made within a very short time frame, and with a circumscribed amount of information. After all, there is limited time and resources available for high-level executives to make these decisions. What this means is that most pitching scenarios are decided by a first impression - and that first impression is strongly affected by how compelling of a story you can tell. The best part is: I can guarantee that you already have a compelling story to tell! The hard work comes in how to convey this story to your interviewer in a way that highlights the value you bring to the table during an executive interview.

In this book, I provide some guidance, taken from my experience in executive interview coaching, for how to frame the introduction of your pitch appropriately and how to get and keep attention (and therefore control) during the pitching process. I touch on both what you say and how you should say it; in other words, not only the content of the pitch, but your non-verbal communication and speaking style, which will strongly predispose your audience to either dismiss you out of hand, or hang on to your every word.

Remember that your compelling story - the one that will land you your next executive opportunity - is already inside you. We just need to package it appropriately for consumption. We are in a world where the rate of change is so fast that you have to continuously re-tool yourself just to remain relevant; that's why the most essential skill to success in any hidden job interview scenario is the ability to pitch yourself successfully. I hope that this book will bring you new insights into the process of both formulating as well as delivering your Perfect Pitch!

Part 1

PITCH CONTENT

The Goal of Your Pitch

Contrary to conventional interviewing wisdom, the goal of an interview pitch is not to get an offer or to get hired, but rather to move forward to the next interview (in other words, to the next round of the conversation).

Because executive-level interviews take several rounds, you must pitch with the aim of securing for yourself a spot in a second-round interview. During the second interview, you will then pitch with the aim of moving forward to the third-round interview, and so on. Another way to think about this is that you must leave a lasting enough impression that the interviewer becomes an advocate for you during decision-making processes, when you will not be around to personally make your case for inclusion in the second round of interviews.

Whether you are trying to get hired outright or move to the next round of interviews, however, the goal is to compel your listener (in this case, the interviewer) *to take action*. You must transform yourself from just another *résumé* on the pile into someone with a compelling work history - someone who is the essential choice for the job.

> **THE GOAL OF YOUR PITCH IS TO COMPEL YOUR LISTENER TO TAKE ACTION**

Telling a compelling story

You've probably seen enough pitches in a business environment to know that having the best product or being the best candidate is not enough to make a sale or land the job. Rather, the *story that accompanies your pitch* is integral to its success.

Think of Steve Jobs in October of 2001, when he introduced the world to the iPod. The iPod was a phenomenal, well-constructed device. However, portable music was nothing new: the original Sony Walkman had been released in 1979, and MP3 players had been on the market since 1998. Moreover, an MP3 player with a larger-capacity hard drive, the Creative Nomad Jukebox, had already been released one year before the iPod.

So, how did Jobs convince millions of people to link Apple Inc. and music forever in their minds? The answer is that he wasn't selling you just another MP3 player; he was selling you *"1,000 songs in your pocket."* In other words, he told a story that was laser-focused on the value offered by his product. The iPod not only overtook the competition, but went on to become the best-selling electronics entertainment product in history.

The Success of Your Pitch

Think back on the most compelling, persuasive arguments you've ever heard; as the advertising specialist Jon Steel writes, you probably didn't hear them in a conference room presentation!

So what does a successful pitch look like? Let's think for a moment about its essential elements.

By definition, a successful pitch moves the interviewer to take action in the desired direction. In your case, this can be a second interview, an introduction to an important decision-maker, or an invitation to wine and dine or to some other event. What all of these have in common is that they require the interviewer to make the next move. Much like a sales pitch, which relies on the customer making a decision (to purchase or pay for an item or service), all that matters is whether the interviewer is moved to act in response to your pitch.

The quality of the interviewer's action is the best mark of your pitching success. In other words, all that matters is what the interviewer does in response to your pitch. No matter what you say or how you say it, what is essential is the interviewer's reaction. No matter how proud you are of your diction and your non-verbals (which require a lot of effort to optimize), success happens when the interviewer is compelled to do something and move your agenda forward one step.

So how do you get the interviewer to take action, and how do you know whether you are successful?

The answer is that you must engage the interviewer in order to provide new commercial or technical insights and to make them say, "Tell me more about it!" This is one sign you are on the right track. The good thing is that at this stage of your career, you have likely made successful pitches from time to time; remember that you have what it takes to be a perfect pitcher all the time! You just need practice and consistency.

Breaking Through the *Status Quo*

The *status quo* is your greatest enemy; when the *status quo* reigns supreme, the interviewer does not act in response to your pitch.

I like to think of the *status quo* as organizational inertia: think of all the ways your organization itself may be difficult to change. The causes underlying inertia may seem trivial at times, but they can be a sign that an organization is ready for a *status quo* breakthrough. Siemens took ages to decide whether wireless communication chips should belong to the Wireless Division or the Automotive Division. Sony spent 1 to 2 years discussing whether they are an electronics or entertainment company, without reaching a consensus. As a result, they could not agree on a new CEO until, eventually, they appointed Sir Howard Stringer from their US business in 2005, the first and only foreigner to ever hold Sony's top job.

Stringer did not even speak any Japanese, but was considered a neutral choice, in order to appease the two opposing electronics-vs-entertainment-industry forces at the board level. In other words: Sony made a safe, conservative (and arguably sub-optimal) choice in order to maintain the *status quo*, largely driven by organizational inertia caused by an inability to choose between two competing visions for the company.

Managers, executives, and employees up and down the organizational structure are used to doing things a certain way, and they are likely working at or near 100% capacity already. When we ask them to change, we are asking them to put in extra time - which they likely don't have - in order to modify their way of thinking or behavior. Changing the *status quo*, then, is an energy-intensive process that requires serious attention and motivation.

> **A GOOD PITCH IS LIKE A TRIGGER, MOVING THE SWITCH FROM OFF TO ON, FROM OLD TO NEW, FROM GOOD TO BETTER, AND FROM BETTER TO BEST.**

The power of the pitch is to set in motion a process that ultimately changes the *status quo*. The change agent, though, is *you*: your unique solution is the trailblazing element that the interviewer is considering with a risk-avoidance attitude.

Let us not forget that another ongoing change in the corporate world is the appointment of more female executives. If you are a female executive, you should absolutely strike the iron while it is hot and pitch with confidence, given that only 8% of Fortune 500 companies have female CEOs[1]. In 2021, equitable hiring is hotter than ever before, with no signs of stopping. The appointment of Karen Lynch at CVS Health in the US or Belén Garijo at conglomerate Merck in Germany are notable appointments in 2021.

These days, then, just getting more women on board in male-dominated industries such as automotive, robotics, oil

---

[1] See, for example, Emma Hinchcliffe, "The female CEOs on this year's Fortune 500 just broke three all-time records," *Fortune*, June 2, 2021.

& gas, or construction can mean breaking the *status quo*. As a recent example, VW interviewed a female McKinsey executive-turned-government official as well as the female Head of IT at notoriously slow-moving Deutsche Bahn in 2021. Both candidates had no automotive experience whatsoever, and internally, VW had multiple male CIO candidates lined up with perfect backgrounds. What can we learn from this? If you are a female candidate, you have a competitive advantage that you should exploit to help break the *status quo*.

However difficult it can be, breaking the *status quo* is necessary to success during the interview process. When you succeed in shattering the *status quo*, you have the opportunity to change the mind of your interviewer, bring them on board to your point of view, and ideally to act as your surrogate behind closed doors. To cause your interviewer to perk up and listen, you must supply them with something that will be worth the trouble of breaking the *status quo*: you must offer them novel solutions and irresistible value.

Old School vs. New School of Pitching

This focus on novel, irresistible value is at the heart of what I refer to as the New School of pitching. The pitching style exemplified by the New School parallels an analogous shift in sales techniques that have occured over the last twenty years from simple, transactional sales to complex, solutions-based sales techniques.

Let's consider an example from the Old School of pitching; this characterizes most of the interviewing scenarios today. The typical applicant, even at the executive level, is more often than not a passive participant in the interview process: they are called in for an interview, hoping that the interviewer will see their potential as the ideal candidate on their own. Because of this, they believe that, as long as they don't make big mistakes during the interview process and demonstrate that they fulfill the application criteria, they will get the position.

The Old School of pitching is characteristic of the old style of transactional sales: it is centered on passive techniques, in which you regurgitate your *résumé* at the decision-maker and wait around for a call back. By contrast, the New School excels at taking control of the pitch and providing novel and exciting solutions to the decision-maker, attempting to drive a decision before the end of the pitch.

Above all other interview scenarios, the Old School approach does not apply in the Hidden Job Market. Above all else, the Hidden Job Market is a seller's market: you have something to offer as an executive, and are looking for the perfect buyer who will pay (i.e. give you a salary) for that value. Therefore, it is not enough to come away from the interview without having rocked the boat and left a negative impression; you must provide direct evidence of how you will contribute to the organization's success better than all the other candidates. In other words: you must offer irresistible value.

Irresistible Value

In order for your pitch to land perfectly, you must offer irresistible value to the interviewer. You must make clear, as quickly as possible, that you are worthy of their investment, in terms of time, attention, and eventually money.

To do this, you must identify the value you offer (as perceived by the interviewer) and then use this knowledge to guide you in breaking past their expectations by offering something that, while offering tangible and clear value (i.e. a solution to a problem they face) is both novel and exciting.

Both elements are essential: if you offer them a novel and exciting solution to a problem the interviewer doesn't care about or can't imagine happening to them, you will miss the mark, scoring no points. On the other hand, if you offer something good but predictable, you will fail to break through the *status quo*.

Perfect Control, Perfect Pitch: The Illusion of the Perfect Candidate

Without maintaining control of the direction and momentum of the interview, however, you will never have a chance to make your irresistible value proposition: controlling the interview not only ensures maximum attention, but also protects you throughout the interview process. Why is this?

Have you ever read a job or position description and felt discouraged, thinking that you may be missing key skills asked for in the job specifications? It almost seems as if the company placing the advertisement can picture exactly who they are looking for - and it sure doesn't look like it's you!

The truth, of course, is that this description is only an illusion - there is no perfect candidate out there. Put more precisely, there is no *perfect* candidate; the *best choice* candidate, however, *can* be you! The interviewer knows this, and you also must be aware of it when going into the interview process. This is not just an issue of morale; you must be prepared for the possibility that the interviewer may be looking to test your limits and to find your flaws. It is crucial to maintain control of the interview's momentum: with this, you can prevent (or at least limit) the interviewer's ability to derail your pitch by shifting the focus to a topic you are less comfortable with or to a less stellar part of your *résumé*.

In the following section, we will discuss how to structure your pitch in order to grab control of the interview and maintain attention on the facets of your pitch that you are most excited to share with the interviewer. Maintaining focus on your vision, and thus maintaining control of the process, is how you will truly shine during your pitch!

Part 2

THE STRUCTURE OF A PITCH

To be successful during your pitch, you must be organized, because you will need to balance two things: control of the conversation as well as the attention of the interviewer.

For some people, maintaining the attention of even a crowd of people comes naturally. Street performers, people in show-business, and rock stars make it look effortless, but chances are they are working hard behind the scenes to ensure success. Ask them about how they do it, and they may tell you that they have strategies for how to keep the audience's attention. They may deploy particular strategies at the beginning or throughout their performance; they may avoid particular things that they know, from experience, will kill interest in their act.

Ask ten performers, and they may give you ten different answers for how they do this. However, the unifying thing will be that they all have *a system*. In other words, they don't approach attention control at random, but use a process designed to maximize success. In this section, I will outline for you one such process, which will help you to organize your pitch and maximize your ability to maintain attention.

Before we do this, however, it can be helpful to first look at an example of a "poor pitch." After we outline the necessary elements of a good pitch and describe them in detail, we can then return to this "poor pitch" and think about how we can modify it to turn it into a good (or at least, a much better) pitch.

The Four Elements of a Good Pitch

Any pitch that doesn't engender the desire for action is a poor pitch on the part of the interviewer. Unfortunately, poor pitches are absolutely endemic in the current business climate, even at the executive level. Let's look at the following example:

> Interviewee: *Good afternoon; I'm happy to get a chance to talk to you. I am French, married with three children. I have more than twenty years of HR experience in a tech company. I have had the chance to work and live in different locations across the US and Europe, and had the opportunity to work with different functions from R&D to manufacturing, as well as had the chance to successfully work with different senior leaders.*

Would you be moved to action by this sales pitch? It's very unlikely! It is missing many aspects of what makes for a good pitch; because of this, it fails to break through the *status quo* and drive the interviewer to take action. Among other problems with this pitch example, the sales pitch focuses on checking boxes rather than differentiating the interviewee from the competition. More importantly, however, it is missing several essential elements at the heart of the Perfect Pitching system.

The four essential components of a pitch, according to this system, are the following:

1. The Hook
2. The Introduction
3. The Content
4. The Call to Action

The Hook, one of the most powerful arrows in your quiver, draws the audience in; *The Introduction*, lays the groundwork for your pitch to succeed by succinctly and effectively giving the necessary background for your pitch; *The Content*, which is where your pitch fully blossoms, provides the evidence to convince the interviewer of your value; and finally, *The Call to Ac-*

tion, where you summarize your pitch succinctly in such a way that the interviewer is encouraged to take a concrete action.

The good news: you already have an incredible story waiting to be told, and your career is full of evidence that demonstrates your incredible abilities and skills! If you are less charismatic or not much of a natural storyteller, don't despair; a little time and planning will help you to hammer out a good Hook to draw in your audience and a Call to Action that lands well.

Similar to the example above, however, it can be very illuminating to look at some examples of how a poorly-designed pitch can fail to deliver on each of these items. This will help you to avoid particular pitfalls. To better picture these further examples of poor pitches, I'll introduce three characters who will deliver them, and we will then sprinkle excerpts from their pitches throughout this chapter. Our players are:

- **"The Pharma VP":** A 50-year-old pharmaceutical/biomedical, PhD-educated Vice President of Clinical Development and Strategy pitching themselves to a top biotechnology company, which is expanding its business drastically during the Covid-19 pandemic. Their pitch is decently balanced in terms of content, but the delivery falls short and misplaces important elements of the pitch, as we shall see.

- **"The Cybersecurity CEO":** A mid-30s CEO of a mid-sized cybersecurity company, pitching themselves to a leading technology company. As we will see, they drastically undersell themselves and miss many essential elements in their pitch, destroying any chance of being considered for the next round of interviews.

- **"The Head of Strategy":** A mid-40s Head of Strategy with a $1 million salary, pitching themselves (and their substantial expertise and experience) to a multinational computing firm. Their extreme confidence, when combined with several missing essential elements of the pitch, backfires and severely damages their delivery of the Call to Action.

Let's take a look at each of the essential items of a pitch in turn, and discuss the mistakes made by each of our "poor pitchers."

First: The Hook

The goal of the hook is to grab your interviewer's attention, so that you can pitch with the highest impact. Think of attention as an inverted filter: the less attention you have, the fuzzier your image will be for the observer. When you maximize attention, however, you convey a crystal-clear, high-definition image to the observer, maximizing the chances that your pitch will be received as you intend it, or that it is even received at all!

> **NO HOOK, NO ATTENTION. NO ATTENTION. NO IMPACT, INTERVIEW LOST.**

The idea of the hook comes from consumer advertisements, like infomercials or TV ads. Catching the audience's attention is necessary, otherwise there is no one listening to the brand message that follows. Every bit of attention lost costs you dearly, and yet you cannot maintain attention indefinitely; you must therefore use the hook to create an opening within which you have the highest possible chance of your message being received.

8 Seconds Attention Span

According to a 2015 Consumer Insights Team report by Microsoft Canada, people tend to lose attention after listening to something for longer than 8 seconds. This means that your hook must be short and sweet; more than 8 seconds will not always ruin the hook, but stick to the general rule that shorter is better.

Hook With a Question

By their very nature, one of the most powerful ways to grab someone's attention is to ask a question. Questions imply a request for an answer, and thus are naturally engaging.

Here is a short list of possible questions:

Have you noticed that...?

You know how...?

Doesn't it seem like...?

I'll never forget the time when...

Would you like to hear about a "Mission Impossible" turn-around?

Whatever the question you use for your hook, you must be prepared to follow it with meaningful content that drives home the message of your pitch in the hard-earned but brief period during which you will have your interviewer's undivided attention.

If you don't have a hook, you therefore risk losing the attention of your interviewer right when you get to the good stuff (in other words, your Introduction and your Content). If you can't hook them for those details, your Call to Action will fail completely, because the interviewer won't be convinced about why they should change the *status quo* by bringing you on board.

To see the power of a good hook, it is illustrating to think about our three "poor pitchers."

The Pharma VP:

> *"It is great to meet you. So, a little about myself: I have been in the pharma and biotech industry for 20 years, and I have always been passionate about making things happen. That is what really drives me. The speed of change and the speed that things move is..."*

As we can see, The Pharma VP fails to deliver a Hook, instead providing some basic biographical details before moving into their pitch. Interestingly, we find that there is a nice Hook in their pitch - it just happens to be buried deep, much later in their delivery:

> *"If you look at the way we operate clinical trials in the industry, it has not really changed over the last 50 years. At the same time, technology has developed, and things have incrementally improved. My approach, fundamentally, is to start from scratch and to ask myself: 'Would we really do*

things the same way, if we started from scratch?' And the answer is, absolutely not!"

As you can see, The Pharma VP has a great opportunity to start their pitch from a unique perspective, and with a provocative statement. Instead, they bury this deep inside their pitch; by the time they get here, the interviewer is already snoring, attention has been lost, and it is unlikely to be regained.

The Cybersecurity CEO:

"Have you noticed how these days, most new ideas in our sector are coming from spin-off companies started by dissatisfied former employees? The other day, I ran into one of our best programmers at the farmer's market; we got to talking, and they told me something that almost floored me there and then..."

The Cybersecurity CEO goes on to describe an employee of their firm that similarly left to start a new business with a great idea that hadn't been supported within the company. This provides an excellent Hook, because it immediately connects with the audience: the interviewer also knows about this problem ("brain drain"), and the new company, like most in their sector, is looking for solutions. The Cybersecurity CEO looks like they might have something very interesting to offer!

Unfortunately, the Cybersecurity CEO misses the boat; they don't understand what the Hook's real purpose is. After getting the interviewer's attention, they continue to tell their story about the former employee, wasting valuable time that would be better spent moving on to the next steps of the pitch. By the end of the story, 5 minutes later, the interviewer hasn't learned anything more than what they had already learned in the first 30 seconds of the pitch.

The Head of Strategy:

"Hello Joe, It is an honor to be with you here today. I have been following your career for many years and I have been really amazed by what you have done at Company X. It is

really a pleasure to finally meet you today! I was particularly impressed by what you did at Company X in 2011, when…"

Like the Pharma VP, the Head of Strategy fails to start their pitch with a Hook. Instead, they start their pitch with some platitudes and complements, getting them nowhere and wasting precious time.

As you can imagine, the CEO of Company X (let's call him Joe) is a very busy man, and highly successful. Joe doesn't need the Head of Strategy's praise, and the two of them aren't trading stories at the local pub; he's waiting to hear what the Head of Strategy has to say that will convince him that they're a good fit for the position. Right now, Joe isn't hearing anything at all, and the Head of Strategy's opportunity to get his attention has already slipped away.

Second: The Introduction

Beginning the Pitch

Hooks are important throughout the interview process and throughout your pitch; they will get you out of tricky situations, and prepare the interviewer for a point that can make or break your interview performance.

However, the most critical part of any pitch is in the beginning: this is where the base level of attention and control are set for the entire interview, and thus can determine whether you are fighting uphill or on level ground for the remainder of the interview. This initial process is what I refer to as framing the introduction: you must set the bounds of the interview early, and capture the interviewer's attention.

Framing Your Introduction

The essential job of framing the introduction, after ensuring attention and control, is to disrupt the *status quo* early and to place your value first and foremost in the interviewer's mind.

However, before you can achieve these outcomes, you must first give the interviewer a reason to care about you in particular:

thus, your introduction must answer, as early and succinctly as possible, the crucial question of "Who are you?"

I consider this question to be the conversation icebreaker, telling your interviewer, succinctly, why they should listen to you. The answer to this question consists of your extraordinary solution or the extraordinary value that the interviewer can get from you, while substantiating this value claim by focusing only on the most relevant parts of your background.

The Mini-Mini-Bio As a Glimpse Into Your Background

In the Morita Method, I outline a method for getting the salient points of your career across without regurgitating your entire *résumé* to the interviewer; I call this the mini-bio. In a pitching scenario where you have even less time to spend on your career, however, you need an even more concise version of this; that's what I call the mini-mini-bio.

The mini-mini-bio is about introducing yourself in the most elegant and concise way to the interviewer from a value perspective, much like a movie trailer does for the audience in a theater. It is the bare minimum of information that the interviewer needs to know about you, but with the highest relevance to your value creation claim, and ideally only one to three sentences.

Think about it this way: you start to tell the interviewer a bit about your background and your education; you list off positions and awards, every accomplishment, and after twenty minutes, you've convinced them that you are the greatest hero in the world, right?

Unfortunately, by this point, you've completely lost your audience. No one is interested in hearing about every detail of your career. After all, who has time for that? What you need instead are two or three sentences about yourself, specifically with regard to what the value proposition is that you are bringing to the table. Enough to engender trust, that's all. Minimum number of words, maximum impact.

Let's look again at our three "poor pitchers" to think about what makes a good (and a bad) Introduction.

The Pharma VP:

> *"So, a little about myself: I have been in the pharma and bio-tech industry for 20 years, and I have always been passion-ate about making things happen. That is what really drives me."*

The Pharma VP fails to introduce themselves to the interviewer, not mentioning their company, position, or even their name. Unfortunately, the interviewer doesn't know anything about them; instead of paying attention to their pitch, the interviewer is now (at best) fumbling with papers in front of them for the basic information the Pharma VP failed to mention, or (at worst) has already started to lose interest.

If the interviewer doesn't know who the Pharma VP is, are they even going to remember them after they walk out the door? Don't count on it!

The Cybersecurity CEO:

> *"My name is [name]. I'm a creative solution finder – I like to drive changes, engage people and empower teams to de-velop an agile mindset."*

After their initially effective (but too-long) Hook, the Cybersecurity CEO introduces themselves by name, and gives some key words. Unfortunately, they also miss some key details. Overall, however, the delivery is slightly more effective: the interviewer knows their name, at least.

The Head of Strategy:

> *"I am [name], currently Head of Strategy at ABC multinational B2B company and over the last 20 years of my career I have been building and driving the industry that ABC is in to become more sustainable and to grow our company."*

The Head of Strategy, after their platitudes and complements, introduces themselves effectively and succinctly with the pre-requisite information: name, current position and company are mentioned, and a brief nod to their experience in the field ("20 years of my career...") ensures that the interviewer knows who they are dealing with.

Third: Developing Your Content

> *THOSE WHO TELL STORIES RULE SOCIETY.*
> **-PLATO**

You've hooked the interviewer and laid the groundwork with an introduction that establishes your control and has focused attention on you: now, it is time to actually tell your story. Developing your story's content in an optimal way is essential to a successful pitch, because it provides the evidence that will convince your interviewer to act in response to the final step, the *Call to Action*.

As you will see below, many storytelling formats follow a similar pattern; the goal is not to find the "perfect" storytelling format, but to find the one that best works for you. An ideal storytelling format gives structure to your stories, getting their point across quickly and clearly without wasting your (or the interviewer's) precious time.

Meat on the Bone

Meat on the Bone, another element of the Morita Method, is about supplying proof (the "meat") by giving examples, providing numbers or listing your accomplishments after you have hooked the audience and introduced yourself with your value claim. *Meat on the Bone* as a concept is centered on layering evidence upon the value framework established by your introduction. It is used to quickly express the necessary evidence to back up your overall value claim, and to get to the heart of your qualifications without an exhaustive run through your entire *résumé*.

Without *Meat on the Bone*, the interviewer will get back to you with unexpected and potentially unpleasant questions in order to verify your claims, wasting precious time during your pitch.

> **MAKE IT A PRIORITY TO WOW YOUR INTERVIEWER WITH IMPRESSIVE ACCOMPLISHMENTS.**

In a Perfect Pitching context, *Meat on the Bone* can guide your strategy for fleshing out your pitch. The goal should be to stick to the absolute minimum necessary to convey confidence in your idea, and to provide evidence that your approach will work.

Meat on the Bone keeps you from bloating your pitch with unnecessary detail that will bore your interviewer, and helps to make your pitch more airtight by ensuring that none of your important claims are made without some evidence to back them up. You should keep the concept of *Meat on the Bone* in mind as we explore the two storytelling formats I suggest for developing your content successfully.

Using a Storytelling Format

You may or may not be a natural storyteller; even if you are, the stories you excel at telling may not have the same form and function as the stories you need to tell successfully during a pitch. What you do have, however, is a story to tell. And what you need is an appropriate *storytelling format* that allows this story to do its job: support your pitch with incontrovertible evidence.

The STAR Format

This format stands for Situation, Task, Action, Result, and is commonly taught to MBA students as a means to respond to behavioural interview questions. You probably know the kind well: "What was your biggest failure on the job?", "Describe a time when you utilized your knowledge/experience to solve a problem," and so on.

The STAR format was designed with these questions in mind. In telling a story using this format, you spend a short amount of time describing the Situation you were faced with (to clarify its fit to the interviewer's question), and identify the specific Task you were given. These two expository elements should usually take little more than a quarter of the total time spent on the story; the majority of your time is then spent on the Action section, describing what *you* did, your thought process or rationale for those actions, and finally a short note on the Result.

The CAR Format

The second storytelling format has many similarities with the first. Standing for Challenge (sometimes Context is used instead), Action, Result, This format condenses Situation and Task into one overall phase, which sets the scene for your description of the actions you took to address a particular challenge.

Similarly to the STAR format, the CAR format was designed as a framework for answering behavioural interview questions quickly and successfully. It provides you with a way to quickly get to the heart of the matter and not spend an unnecessary amount of time on exposition or on the downstream effects of your actions.

STAHR: Adapting the STAR format for executives

In the selection process for executives today, you must pay special attention to *how* you achieved particular outcomes; in other words, the transformational aspects of your actions must be clearly highlighted, because they are at the heart of what makes you a great leader (and thus, the ideal candidate for the job). Thus, the STAR/CAR methods, which were designed for MBA student interviews, must be adapted for the executive interview scenario. Let's examine their key elements, and what's missing for executives.

The Situation/Task, Challenge/Context and Result sections cover a rather short amount of your story's time; these are here for context, and to assure the interviewer that you understood the nature of the question. The meat of your story is the Action section, because it gets at what the interviewer wants to know: it clarifies your thought process, how you work, and your problem-solving skills.

During a pitch, you want to get to the heart of your story ⏵ the Action ⏴ as quickly as possible, because this section does the bulk of the convincing. It is the core of *Meat on the Bone*, providing evidence of the claim and backing up the *Call to Action* which will follow in the final section of your pitch. However, here we must modify STAR/CAR, and add something that highlights the transformational aspects of your pitch: the How. This transforms the STAR/CAR format into STAHR/CAHR.

To illustrate the How section, let us look at a real, anonymized example of an executive I prepared for an interview, who described his role in bringing his previous employer, a regional leader in aircraft component manufacture, to profitability.

He sets the scene (Situation/Task/Challenge): the company is highly profitable, but sales are stagnating. A large amount of OEM business has been lost to competitors due to pricing and quality problems, as well as poor reaction times to requests for customization. His goal is to not only demonstrate his ability to win back the lost OEM business, but also to transform the sales team's culture.

He describes the Actions he took to achieve these goals: he focused on high-volume customers and increased turnaround times significantly, and improved quality at a lagging factory by applying an improvement roadmap used at another branch. He also increased market share with key customers through framework agreements. He also increased focus on components that represented business that could be won back without significant retooling at the factory.

Crucially, however, he also expounds impressively on the How; in other words, how was the transformation done, exactly? He describes how this incredible turnaround was achieved by putting in place structural changes: instituting regular communication sessions with the entire team and changing the culture at the sales team from farming current customers to hunting for new ones. He also outlines how he incorporated elements of Scrum, a software development framework that focuses on timeboxed and rapid development and implementation, in order to accelerate responses to customers.

The importance of separating How from Action here is that he demonstrates his ability to institute transformational (and therefore, long-lasting and structural) changes to the work culture in order to get results. At the executive level, how results are achieved matters a great deal; they demonstrate your ability to apply solutions across varied problems in a flexible manner. Make sure to keep a healthy focus on this element of your storytelling by thinking in terms of STAHR/CAHR, not just STAR/CAR.

Learning From Storytelling Formats

Although these tools were designed for reactionary interviewing scenarios (i.e. they assume a behavioral-type question is being asked that must be answered "correctly"), they provide a good framework for developing your pitch because they focus on a few key elements.

The Situation/Task, Challenge/Context and Result sections cover a rather short amount of your story's time; these are here for context, and to assure the interviewer that you understood the nature of the question. The meat of your story is the Action section, because it gets at what the interviewer wants to know: it clarifies your thought process, how you work, and your problem-solving skills.

Similarly, during a pitch, you want to get to the heart of your story - the Action - as quickly as possible, because this is doing the bulk of the convincing in your story. It is the core of *Meat on the Bone*, providing evidence of the claim and backing up the *Call to Action* which will follow in the final section of your pitch.

Don't forget that if you are being invited for an interview, it is because you have (or are expected to provide) a concrete value proposition to the interviewer. All stories you tell must be related to *the value you offer*. Keeping a strict storytelling format in mind will help ensure that your stories stay vinculated to that value proposition.

Let's see what our three "poor pitchers" have to teach us about telling a good story, and what constitutes appropriate Content for your pitch.

The Pharma VP:

> "I am good at a number of things: project management, operational excellence, and more recently, clinical development and clinical trials."

After a laundry list of skills, the Pharma VP jumps into their misplaced Hook, which we have already seen above. However, they don't tell any story at all when talking about their abilities, and provide no *Meat on the Bone* that can convince the interviewer that they actually have the skills they list.

Unfortunately, the lack of Meat on the Bone means that this generic list of skills will be completely ignored by the interviewer; they read all of this in the Pharma VP's *résumé*, and if not, these are standard skills required for the position. There is nothing to make the Pharma VP stand out, and there is no story to illustrate what kind of leadership style or problem-solving the Pharma VP would bring to the table.

The Cybersecurity CEO:

> *"My strengths are that I always keep the big picture focused, and keep my planning long term-oriented and focused on foreseeing losses. I always try to leverage synergy effects and to constantly improve processes, and by doing this I have already reduced development and production costs by 30% at Company Y."*

The Cybersecurity CEO provides what appears, at first, to be some *Meat on the Bone*: they give some hard numbers to back up their claim ("*reduced development and production costs by 30%*").

However, this is just a number thrown around; the interviewer has heard these types of claims before. Moreover, by introducing a sterile number like "*reduced costs by 30% at Company Y,*" the Cybersecurity CEO guarantees that the comparison being made is to another candidate, who claims to have "reduced costs by 45% at Company Z." This reduces the Cybersecurity CEO's excellent track record of problem-solving to a commodity price, and suddenly, they may not look like the best value on the market after all.

The Head of Strategy:

> *"I have experience in all areas of the business. Being a technology native myself, I understand the broader outlook and the perspective in the sector. I really look forward to a conversation with you on how I can bring these skills to the company, grow and expand in those areas, and build the business. Growing the business, growing profits. In other words, doing well by doing good."*

Like our other "poor pitchers," the Head of Strategy fails to tell a story that provides evidence of their abilities. Instead, they make broad claims that are taken straight from their *résumé*, and fail to substantiate those claims with a vivid story that will be remembered later on by the interviewer.

Another grave mistake made by the Head of Strategy is to offer to continue the conversation later at this point. They have yet to provide any enticement for the interviewer to take the conversation further, and so this offer falls flat on its face.

Fourth: The Call to Action

The *Call to Action* is an essential element of your pitching strategy; without it, your pitch ends without a powerful final blow, and no decision has been made. You leave the interview with nothing having been gained, similar to how you arrived; don't let this happen to you!

The *Call to Action* is about avoiding being passive; you should transform yourself instead into an "active seller" on your own behalf. Don't expect others to ask you "the right questions," because you will be waiting in vain! Create opportunities for yourself instead to demonstrate your value.

Likewise, when it comes to closing your pitch, you cannot wait for the interviewer/interviewer to be inspired on their own, but need to create opportunities to capitalize on your effective storytelling. There are a few elements that are essential to getting your interviewer to take action on your pitch.

Inspire the Interviewer to Act

Think about what moves you to take action: what gets you out on a run, or to take your family to the beach or to the mountains? Inspiration can be a powerful driving force behind a *Call to Action*.

That means you should consider your interviewer's reaction to your storytelling carefully: zero in on the elements of your pitch that most seem to inspire them. Find what inspires the interviewer, and you will probably find what solutions they are most looking for.

Never forget: by definition, you are pitching to an interviewer that has multiple options at their disposal, and you are only one of these options. Your best chance of walking away with a new position, after making your value proposition and backing it up with *Meat on the Bone*, is to make a *Call to Action* that gets you a response before the interview is over. Deferring the decision keeps other options on the table for the interviewer, which decreases your chances of success.

As our final step in looking at the four essential elements of a pitch, let's look at how our "poor pitchers" make their final case to the interviewer.

The Pharma VP:

> "I am very excited to be part of the conversation, and to potentially pass on my experience, but also to keep learning. I think that is another area that I have really enjoyed during my career. It is about two-way learning and sharing of information; that really excites me."

The Pharma VP fails to provide a strong *Call to Action* for the interviewer, instead giving them a rather generic and obvious closing statement ("*I am excited to be a part of the conversation*") without making any final case that would get the interviewer to act.

The Cybersecurity CEO:

> *"I look forward to the opportunity to test my abilities further and to empower your teams at Company X. If you think I can be of help to you in the next phase of your business, I will be eagerly awaiting your call."*

Unlike the Pharma VP, the Cybersecurity CEO appears to make a *Call to Action*: if you think I am your guy, I'll be waiting for you to contact me. Unfortunately, it is very weak, because it doesn't move the interviewer to act on anything specific. Instead, it provides a nebulous request and leaves the decision of whether the Cybersecurity CEO is the right person for the job to be made later, when they are out of the room.

The *status quo* remains utterly unmoved, and the interviewer mentally moves to the next candidate before the Cybersecurity CEO is even out the door.

The Head of Strategy:

> *"Tell the board that you ran into someone special; someone who can help you grow this area of the business. I can help you bring this area of the business to unimaginable heights in terms of what we do for our customers, and to help you act on unmet needs. And tell them that I am the right guy for you to make that happen; to grow and change the game in the market."*

Unlike our other two examples, the Head of Strategy makes a clear and strong *Call to Action*. In other words, they call on the interviewer to take a very specific action ("*Tell the board...*"), and they make a strong claim about their abilities (the interviewer *did* run into someone special, rather than asking the interviewer, "*if you* think *you ran into someone special...*").

Sadly, despite this clear *Call to Action*, the Head of Strategy has not provided the *Content* and *Meat on the Bone* to back up their strong claims; because of this, the *status quo* similarly remains unbroken, because the interviewer is not convinced about the validity of these claims.

Turning a Poor Pitch Into a Good One

Now that we know the elements of a good pitch, we can go back and evaluate what was missing from our "poor pitch" example earlier on. You should now be able to identify that this pitch is missing each of the components discussed above: a hook, an effective introduction, content development, and a call to action:

> *I am French, married with three children. I have more than twenty years of HR experience in a tech company. I have had the chance to work and live in different locations across the US and Europe, and had the opportunity to work with different functions from R&D to manufacturing, as well as had the chance to successfully work with different senior leaders.*

If we add a basic version of each of the elements discussed above, we may arrive at something like the following:

> *I'll never forget my most challenging experience with HR, at the leading tech company where I have worked for the last twenty years. I had recently moved to the US branch after 7 years working across various cultures in Europe; I wasn't accustomed to the different approach to HR in the US. I realized after a few days that my extensive experience solving problems in manufacturing actually would provide a great framework for solving my problem with the R&D branch, and the senior contacts I had made in the European branches provided me with great feedback for how to address these issues. Given the challenges your operation is currently facing, I am sure that experience will serve me well in addressing your needs.*

Regardless of whether this is a *good* pitch, it is certainly a *better* pitch than the one above. To maximize the chances of success, a pitch requires the four elements of a *Hook*, a succinct

Introduction (with a compelling story), relevant *Content* (i.e. *Meat on the Bone*) and a convincing *Call to Action*.

Getting the structure and the elements of your pitch right is an essential step in constructing a successful pitch. As you will see in the following chapters, you must practice your delivery (both its content and the non-verbal elements of your pitch, such as body language) to maximize your success; however, there's not much you can do if you are not working with the right structure and components in the first place!

Part 3:

NON-VERBAL COMMUNICATION

You may have heard that 93% of all human communication is non-verbal. While the specific percentage has varied from study to study, experts generally agree that a vast amount of the information content conveyed by interpersonal communication comes from non-verbal cues such as tone and body language.

You've prepared your pitch perfectly, memorizing all of your most salient points and generating an exciting introduction to your pitch. Five minutes in, you notice the decision-maker or interviewer's eyes are glazing over, and you're losing their attention. What happened?

You've spent hours thinking about your pitch's content, and years honing your skills and becoming a world-class executive or executive candidate. Trust your message and its contents! Before tinkering with anything else, you should investigate the possibility that non-verbal communication cues are to blame.

It's Not What You Say, But How You Say It

Many studies have highlighted the power of *how* you say things to radically change how your message is perceived. In one of the most notable examples to date, Prof. Albert Mehrabian, in his 1971 book *Silent Messages*, found that when there is an inconsistency between a speaker's words, voice and body language, people tend to ascribe only 7% of meaning to the words themselves. In other words, 93% of people's understanding comes from voice and body language, with an incredible 55% of understanding coming just from facial expression alone. Most people, however, neglect the importance of their voice and demeanor when introducing themselves.

Strictly speaking, what connects you with others is your voice. When trying to improve the quality of your vocal delivery, therefore, the three most important things to keep in mind are the tone, pacing, and rhythm of your speech. Modulating these three carefully for maximum effect can give you an edge in both winning and maintaining attention during your pitch.

Warm Tone, Warm Reception

Tone, or inflection, involves the use of pitch to communicate different emotional values. If you have a pet dog at home, you likely already grasp how powerful tone can be. Say to the same dog, in a happy voice, "Good boy!" or "Bad dog!" and you will likely receive the same happy wag of the tail. Likewise, the same words spoken in a cold tone of reproach will likely sound like a punishment and yield the expected response.

You may be surprised to learn that humans are not so different from dogs in this regard. In one study, researchers found that communicating words with positive, negative, or neutral tones could completely change how interviewers rated the word, regardless of what the word actually meant.

The warmth of your tone thus can do an incredible amount to help engage your interviewer; likewise, a cold or robotic tone can easily lead to glances at the clock, suppressed yawns, or outright hostility from your interviewer. Make sure that you keep your tone as warm as possible in order to maximize your likeability and build bridges between yourself and the interviewer.

Pace and Rhythm: Keep It Varied

Another important non-verbal aspect of your pitch is the pacing or rhythmicity of your speech. It is essential to vary pace and rhythm in order to generate forward momentum in your pitch and maintain attention (and thus command) of the room.

By varying your speed and articulation, you should seek to sound as authentic as possible and to maintain control of your delivery. A more common danger is speeding up your delivery, which may cause you to leave your audience behind as well as to potentially make costly verbal blunders that damage your credibility. Many people speed up their delivery subconsciously when they are nervous; remember to be decisive and to trust your content! Slow down and let the interviewer truly hear what you have to say.

Body Language

Alongside pacing and tone control, body language has the potential to both cement key points as well as cripple your delivery by distracting the interviewer at a critical moment.

Executives often neglect to pay attention to their hands. In my training sessions with executives the world over, I have noticed that the great majority - perhaps 8 or 9 in 10 of them - play with a pen while sitting at a table. Some also may engage in other forms of distracting body language. Fidgeting with your fingers is another example. You must avoid this at all costs during your pitch, as it significantly detracts from the power of your delivery and from how authoritative you sound.

On the other hand, body language can become a great aid; you can use your hands to emphasize key points and as a focal point for the interviewer's attention, such as by utilizing the "teacher's finger:" a single finger held upright to emphasize specific parts of your pitch. However, be extremely careful to never point at your interviewer, as you may come across as patronizing or even threatening.

Become an Authentic Leader

Taking care of how you present yourself to your interviewer (your tone, pacing, and body language) is all about contributing to your image of authenticity. It is imperative that the interviewer see you as an authentic leader, since this will help to support your value offer and the Meat on the Bone offered as evidence.

To maintain authenticity, there are a few crucial things to keep in mind. For example, you must be careful to know when you have already won maximum effect with your pitch.

Many sales techniques books from the Old School call on you to close aggressively and to "not take no for an answer." It's not clear that this advice ever really made much sense; however, if it did it was likely only in an environment akin to the door-to-door sale: your audience may run away or shut the door in your face at any moment, so you need to force a deal somehow as quickly as possible.

However, when you have a voluntary audience that has given you their valuable time and attention to hear your pitch, this advice is dangerously wrong. It is best to make your pitch carefully while maintaining control of the direction of the conversation and wait for the right moment to strike.

Only then, when you see the arguments you have made are sinking in and buy-in and consensus are circling around your idea, should you close firmly and confidently to seal the deal.

Humor

You can also feel free to use some light humor throughout your pitch to better engage with your interviewer and build rapport. Humor, when used appropriately, can improve your ability to maintain attention throughout the pitch. The use of humor, however, is depending on the cultural context. There are certain countries which have a "stricly-business-no-jokes" culture such as Sweden, Finland or Japan just to mention a few.

Humor can also help to generate familiarity with your audience, and thus increase the chance of a positive reception to your pitch. Another great advantage of using humor is that it may help you to relax and enjoy the process itself; a happy, confident pitcher is attractive and much more likely to be listened to!

Genuine Smile

The shortest connection between two people is a smile. Whenever I observe executives presenting their pitch to me, I see their dead serious faces. Stiff. Tense. They are so deeply immersed into their pitch, they completely forget to empathize. Your genuine smile indicates the interviewer that you are comfortable with yourself. A true smile indicates that you are confident in your abilities. Do not miss out on the magic of your smile!

At this stage, I caution you that in different cultures in the world smiles have different meaning such as Russia or Japan and therefore you are better off not to smile.

Cognitive Bias

Nobody is perfect. We tend to trust leaders more easily who openly share their weaknessess. Let us talk about unconscious bias which negatively affects anyone. There are many cognitive biases you need to be aware of to be the best version of you. Here are three examples: We place higher value on things we partially created ourselves. We don't think we have bias, and we see it in others more than ourselves. We sometimes are over-optimistic about good outcomes.

What matters is that in an interview you can create an authentic story about your bias which cultivates a deeper level of connection and trust between you and the interviewer. Name the bias and how you overcame the bias or are planning to overcome it when it appears next time.

Own The Room

By combining effective non-verbal cues and speech modulation with the contents of a winning pitch, you can maintain attention and "own" the room.

These non-verbal tools for owning the room also extend to other aspects of how you present yourself, such as your dress and posture. Your audience will make subconscious and near-instantaneous judgments of your trustworthiness and reliability from the moment they lay eyes on you; you must therefore dress in a way that conveys effortless confidence.

"Dressing to impress" covers a wide range of possibilities, and executives are likely to have developed a sense of self-image that will be appropriate for the pitch you are making. It is important to think about the interactive effect of your style of dress with your other non-verbal cues. As an example, heavy top-framed glasses combined with a certain style of hand gestures may come across as arrogant or patronizing, even when this is against your intentions.

By taking care to think about your non-verbal communication style as a whole, and how different elements interact to yield a particular perception, you can maintain control of the flow of the conversation and maximize the power of your pitch.

Tips for Video Interviewing

Owning the room can seem difficult to do in our new age of virtual interviewing. However, there are some crucial tips that can help keep attention on you and focus on the aspects of your pitch that you seek to highlight.

Being in a video interview is a bit like auditioning for a role. More than being about getting the role, auditioning is about turning the casting director into your biggest fan; after the audition, you have little to no control over what happens. You must strive to leave a good impression in the time you have.

Just like a professional actor, make yourself the person that people will want to work with by not only getting familiar with the lines, but also by tailoring your presentation and positioning for the camera — in other words, the technical aspects of succeeding in a video interview are just as important as the content of your pitch.

Setting the Stage

It is imperative that you make the best first impression that you can, even in a video interview. Much as you would never dream of attending an in-person interview in your pajamas and slippers, you must take care that the first impression you project to the interviewer is one of professionalism and competence.

Thus, ensure that your Twitter, Zoom, or other screen name and photo/avatar are professional and appropriate, as these will be the very first things about you that the interviewer will see (aside from your *résumé*). You should also take care to keep your background neutral and professional; don't be afraid to make use of artificial backgrounds in order to ensure consistency without requiring an entire redecorating session in your interviewing space.

Aside from aesthetic considerations, you should take care to check your technology in advance, as well; poor audio and video quality and faulty connections can spell doom for your pitch. If the interviewer can't hear or see you properly, they can't be impressed by what you have to say, and are likely to be distracted and irritated instead of thinking about your great ideas for the organization.

Body Language Is Still Critical, Even Online

By now, most of us have had many online meetings; haven't you noticed when one of your colleagues was toying with an item at their desk, or clearly reading or otherwise disengaged with the conversation? Don't make the mistake of thinking that your interviewer cannot see exactly what you are doing, or how you are presenting yourself. Make use of positive body language by smiling, maintaining eye contact, using hand gestures as appropriate to emphasize your points, and nodding along and otherwise communicating that you are following the conversation.

The "3 Minutes and 30 Seconds" Rule of Video Interviews

Usually, the time to answer a video interview question will depend on the nature of the question being asked. It may take an average of 45 seconds to answer simple questions, such as "How did you hear about this position?," while behavioral questions such as "Tell us about a time when you worked under pressure, and how you navigated through it," should take about 3 minutes to answer, depending on your talking speed.

The golden rule for answering video interview questions is to talk slowly and wrap up your answer within a maximum of 3 minutes; the extra 30 seconds serve as a pause for your interviewer to process your answers and prepare the next question. Anything beyond 3 minutes is too long; this will bore the interviewer cause them to lose the thread of answer.

Of course, this is a guideline; exceeding 3 minutes doesn't automatically translate into failure. However, you may want to avoid a situation where the interviewer has to cut you off, or ask you to repeat something you said at the beginning. Some interviewers may take answer length very seriously, and judge you based on your ability to talk just long enough, without having short, snippy answers or long-winded, boring ones. Since you likely won't know what their opinion on answer lengths is, it's best to stay on a safe side and stick to the "3 minutes, 30 seconds" rule.

Remember that video interview preparation is 90% preparation and just 10% perspiration. It's almost never a good idea to simply go off the cuff and engage in a conversation. Instead, memorize your script, study your role, and passionately rehearse your delivery – that way, you'll be closer to being the person who gets the part!

Part 4

HOW TO GET THE PERFECT PITCH PERFECTLY RIGHT

Having a perfect pitch (including the nonverbal part) planned is one thing - however, actually delivering that "perfect pitch" perfectly is a matter of practice and ultimately delivery.

As you will see below, there are several things that are essential to a perfect pitch delivery. These have partially to do with your mindset - both in terms of confidence and in an unwavering desire to get to that flawless delivery.

Practice Makes Perfect

Although it may seem like an old cliché, the hard truth is that practice and preparation are essential to improving your ability to deliver a perfect pitch.

Of course, there are more or less painful ways to practice that delivery; although they are often lessons you never forget, it is best to avoid learning through real-world failure when possible. To do that, you must practice your pitch *before* it is ever delivered in the high-stakes environment of a boardroom or interview chamber.

Practice With Video

One of the most powerful ways to modify your non-verbal communication style, and to catch any elements that clash with how you are hoping to present yourself, is to use video recordings. There is simply no substitute for video when it comes to getting a better feeling for your non-verbal communication.

To begin with, choose a smaller section of your overall pitch, perhaps your introduction, or else a part that you have thought about carefully and believe you can explain convincingly. Record yourself delivering this segment of your pitch in a well-lit space, in a way that reflects the perspective of your audience and affords a nice view of your arms and any gestures you may be making.

Keep this exercise short - no more than three minutes, and ideally less. The goal is to look for signs regarding your non-verbal communication. How fast are you speaking? Do you vary your tone and rhythm in a way that is interesting and natural? What manner of hand gestures do you use? Do you find yourself playing with a pen, or resting your face on your hand while talking?

These are all great starting points to work on by using video practice sessions. Remember that you may need to do this again and again in order to discover any wider patterns of behavior. Try to be as critical as possible of your own non-verbal style; only then will you stand a chance of making the changes necessary to succeed.

By thinking about these various questions and observing how you look when you are communicating your pitch, you can be better prepared to modify your behavior as appropriate in order to maximize your ability to own any room during a pitch.

Practicing STAR/CAR storytelling

Here is a useful exercise to practice your delivery during the interview: First, get yourself a stack of flashcards, so that you are not tempted to write entire sentences on them. Now, think about your greatest challenges from your career that you succeeded in overcoming.

On each card, you will answer three questions with the fewest number of words; ideally, one word should suffice per question. These questions are: what was the challenge/problem? How did you solve it? And what was the final result or outcome? What can you do for us? Write the answers to each of these on the same card per challenge.

Now, make a separate stack of flashcards with typical interview questions. You probably have heard enough of these to be able to produce many examples off the top of your head; otherwise, you can easily perform a web search for most frequently-asked questions in interviews.

Next, shuffle each stack separately and take one card from each; it doesn't matter if the questions are unlikely to be asked in your interview scenario, or if they don't fit well to the example challenges you drew; in fact, the less they fit, the better! The important thing is that you practice. The important point is to ensure that you answer each question by outlining your successes succinctly, and that you answer the question on the card explicitly.

By applying this exercise repeatedly, you will both build a repertoire of ready-practiced stories from your career as well as prepare yourself to deliver any story succinctly, even ones you may not have practiced explicitly.

Golden Rules for Perfect Pitching

There are some fundamentals that are essential to any perfect pitch; you must internalize and practice these lessons to have a chance of success.

Many of these lessons are tied to your mindset; both how you approach the content of your pitch as well as how you approach the audience or interviewer who will respond to the pitch once it has been made.

Be Passionate About Your Pitch

Nothing is more off-putting to the people at the receiving end of your pitch than someone who doesn't appear to believe in the success of their own proposal. If you don't 100% believe that your idea will be a smash-hit, why should your audience?

It has been said that some of the best pitches in the world are delivered inside of bars over drinks after a long day at the office. Part of the reason is that this is a collegial environment, where employees can vent their frustrations and share their true opinions about how *they* would have done things differently.

Of course, that doesn't mean the ideas themselves are brilliant; however, their delivery is effective and convincing, in large part because the pitcher is confident in their idea and comfortable with their audience (more on this below). When you pitch your idea, you must similarly remain resolute in the novelty and brilliance of your plan; no one else in the room will be doing that for you!

Know Your Audience

Of course, unlike in the local pub, you are not likely to be intimate friends or perhaps even personally acquainted with your interviewer or audience. However, that doesn't mean you need to walk into your pitch blindly and simply hope for the best. Many people prepare for interviews extensively but completely neglect to research their audience at all.

Today, with the advent of platforms like *LinkedIn* and other professional networks, there is simply no excuse for walking blindly into an interview or any other business meeting. To do so is to willingly walk yourself right into a potential ambush! Although you will be pitching to strangers and the amount of information available will be limited, you must make use of whatever is available in order to leverage as much information about them as possible.

Perhaps your interviewer or audience member has spent a significant portion of their career in a very technical field before entering the executive sphere; on the other hand, they may have climbed their way diligently through their organization's leadership structure to where they are now. You must be aware of their priorities, needs and interests.

The hardest thing in the world is to pitch to complete strangers; it can feel a bit like facing a black hole. Unfortunately this can happen, for example, when executive recruiters do a pre-screen of the first slate of candidates in a confidential search. It may also happen in a Private Equity interview scenario, where you need to sign a confidentiality agreement before the interview and receive little information upfront.

A Little Knowledge Is Sufficient

Part of the beauty of knowing your audience is that you can use these and other pieces of information to tailor your pitch to their interests, as well as to avoid shifting the focus to an area you may not be prepared to receive questions or criticism on.

There is no need to be an expert on everything your pitch touches upon, or on everything that your audience does. In fact, this is a recipe for disaster, as you will never learn enough in the course of a few days or weeks to rival a true expert in their field. Instead, focus on the essentials, and those things that will maximize your impact. Then, use the information you have learned about your audience to keep the conversation focused on the parts of the pitch you articulate best and that resonate most with the audience.

Know how to use Data Storytelling Effectively

Another important consideration is related to what Miro Kaza-koff, Senior Lecturer at MIT Sloan School of Management, refers to as the "Curse of Knowledge." You have spent your career developing innovative solutions to tough, often technical problems; however, the interviewer will not always be an expert in that same area of your business.

You must do your best to remember what it was like *before* you became an expert, and learn how to use data effectively to tell a convincing and compelling narrative. If you fail to do this, you will risk alienating your interviewer and losing their interest in the *Content* of your pitch.

Improving Your Performance With A Sparring Partner

You've thought about your pitch carefully, and even considered your body language and voice in preparation for an interview. Is your pitch already perfect, or is there more you could be doing to prepare?

In order to answer this question and optimize your pitch, you need to enroll someone to help. Just anyone, however, will not suffice; what you need is a sparring partner. Someone who excels at troubleshooting and optimizing. A pitching expert. A "pitch doctor," in other words.

Let's demonstrate the power of a "pitch doctor" or sparring partner with an example from the lesser-known world of book publishing. As I was searching for an expert to help me create a nice layout for the content of my book and to help me design its cover, I read the following advertisement from a graphic design expert:

> "Hello, I am an Art Historian with an MA in Graphic Design, with over 10 years of experience on both book covers and advertising materials. I am specialized in designing eBook covers, paperback and hardcovers, typesetting, and book interior design."

Then I read another pitch, from a freelance graphic designer, which really caught my attention:

> "I am a professional book designer with over 12 years' experience in meeting the aesthetic requirements and marketing needs of the most demanding clients. Having earned rave reviews from new and seasoned authors of every conceivable genre, my unique talent lies in adapting your vision into eye-catching book covers, bleeding-edge designs, clean interior layouts and flawless eBook conversions.
>
> Impress a Large Audience with a Great Book Cover, and Increase Traffic to your social media profile / page with an eye-catching Banner. Order this gig TODAY and EXPAND

your book's readership with Book Cover & Social Media Designs. I look forward to putting your hard work into print!"

Which pitch do you think is better? Most likely, you will agree that it's the second one! Here's a surprise for you: the second candidate is from Russia, and cannot speak English. He officially rates his English skills as "basic." Nonetheless, he comes across well with an excellent pitch that grabs your attention and focuses on the value authors are looking for.

What this means, of course, is that someone else - a "pitch doctor" - has helped him to prepare his pitch. With that assistance, suddenly this relative nobody - a freelancer with no official training in the field - can enter the market and sign deals that would be impossible if he relied solely on his own pitching skills and his incredible talent for designing book covers.

This example illustrates how, in many areas of business, professionals who rely on pitching experts can secure themselves a competitive advantage and make more business - get their foot in the door, or create a door where there was none - than those who do not. After all, as Milton Berle once put it, "if opportunity doesn't knock, build a door."

> *"IF OPPORTUNITY DOESN'T KNOCK, BUILD A DOOR."*
> **-MILTON BERLE**

Some arenas are filled with more natural or better-trained pitchers than others. The worlds of capital-raising, project bids for government funding, Olympic Games bids to the International Olympic Committee are full of these people, for example. The world of executive job interviews, on the other hand, has few pitching experts. That is the reason why I wrote this book: walking hundreds of executives each year through their interview marathons has shown me that they need a job interview pitching expert to get their pitch perfectly right.

Think about how the great athletes prepare for their matches, games, fights, or competitions. Does a great footballer ever simply practice by themselves? Can a boxer prepare for their match without a sparring partner? Much like these individuals, who use sparring partners and coaches to hone their craft and perfect their skills, the only way to truly "up your game" when it comes to perfect pitching and interview success is to find yourself a foil that you can bounce ideas off of and hear feedback from.

No one cares who came up with your pitch, as long as it is compelling and well-delivered. You don't need to master the pitching process on your own, but can rely on the aid of a pitching expert who can guide you through this process.

Unless you have a sparring partner to see and hear you and to give you feedback, you will have a hard time meaningfully improving your technique. You might still improve even without a sparring partner; the question is, however, how long will that take? Do you really have the luxury to find out? As mentioned above, this will mean "trial by combat," in real pitches with real consequences for failure. It's much better to prepare in advance and avoid defeat in battle instead.

CONCLUSION

There are many key elements to prepare when going into an interview scenario or pitch. However, even many diligent interviewees who spend a significant amount of time in interview prep often focus on the wrong targets in anticipation of their pitch.

As I have discussed throughout this book, the key elements that will make or break your pitch are not necessarily the content itself, but how you present the pitch and yourself to your audience, and to what degree you manage to grab and maintain their attention. That is not to say that content is not important, but that you've already taken care of the raw materials of the content with your incredible career- now, you just need to unlock that raw material and turn it into a compelling story that lands your next big job opportunity. To do that, you must get the framing and the conditions of the pitch perfectly down in order to give your exciting ideas a chance for success in the first place.

Controlling the conversation is essential to a successful pitch, because you cannot pitch successfully when you are reacting to the interviewer's or audience's questions and comments. Even if you manage to stave off every possible question and misgiving your audience may have, you will have earned yourself another chance to pitch to them again, at best.

Rather, to have a successful pitch you must get a decision; to get a decision, you must guide the conversation ultimately in that direction, which requires careful control of the conversation and maintaining the engagement and attention of your audience.

I hope that many of the precepts in this book will prove useful to you in your next pitch. Combining a winning idea and the preparation and skillset that this book provides, anyone can deliver a successful pitch. Apply the precepts and the pitch structure I have described, and watch as the quality and impact of your pitch increase - and don't stop until you are delivering the Perfect Pitch!

REFERENCES

Bloomberg L.P. (2021). "BusinessWeek Executive Profile: Howard Stringer". Bloomberg BusinessWeek. URL: https://www.bloomberg.com/profile/person/1394945

Hinchcliffe, Emma (2021). "The female CEOs on this year's Fortune 500 just broke three all-time records." *Fortune*, June 2. URL: https://fortune.com/2021/06/02/female-ceos-fortune-500-2021-women-ceo-list-roz-brewer-walgreens-karen-lynch-cvs-thasunda-brown-duckett-tiaa/

Merck (2021). "Belén Garijo." URL: https://www.merckgroup.com/en/company/management/executive-board/belen-garijo.html

Kazakoff, Miro (2021). "The Curse of Knowledge: Why Experts Struggle to Explain Their Work." *MIT Management Executive Education,* July 21. URL: https://exec.mit.edu/s/blog-post/the-curse-of-knowledge-why-experts-struggle-to-explain-their-work-MCHZYA6AZCFFBGTN6RNH2VBSBWOI

Morita, Rainer Maria (2019). *Find Your Career Passion: Towards Abundant Joy, Fulfillment and Authenticity in Your Job, Career and Life. CreateSpace Publishing, California, USA,* ASIN: B07V32XBQ3.

Morita, Rainer Maria (2019). *Globalization Opportunities for Executives in Japanese Companies. CreateSpace Publishing, California, USA,* ASIN: B07Q2FQSZ1.

Morita, Rainer Maria (2019). *Tokyo Expat Job Search Guide. CreateSpace Publishing, California, USA,* ISBN: 979-12-200-3684-9.

Morita, Rainer Maria (2018). *Executive Job Search in the Hidden Job Market - The Morita Method. CreateSpace Publishing, California, USA,* ISBN-13: 978-151522443.

Morita, Rainer Maria (2018). *Peak Performance Interviewing for Executives. CreateSpace Publishing, California, USA,* ISBN-13: 978-1542893947.

Mehrabian, Albert (1971). *Silent Messages* (1st ed.). Belmont, CA: Wadsworth. ISBN 0-534-00910-7.

DDI World "STAR Method." URL: https://www.ddiworld.com/solutions/behavioral-interviewing/star-method

Leave a Review on Amazon For This Book

Your voice matters. Customer generated word of mouth is more important than ever. Your review helps others to find and buy this book.
If you value this book, leave your Amazon review. Thank you for your cooperation.

UPDATE FOR NEXT EDITION

We welcome your feedback and improvement suggestions to create the next best version of this book for helping other executives be at the edge of their job search game.

What executive or contact would you like to suggest that excels in pitching in executive interviews? What mistake should we correct? Want to share a success story?

Please send an email message with your improvement suggestions addressed to Rainer Morita, contact@HiddenExecutive-Jobs.com

I think that this year's Edition of Perfect Pitching for Executives in the Hidden Job Market needs to be changed in the following way:

_____

_____

_____

_____

Next year's Edition of Perfect Pitching for Executives in the Hidden Job Market should include the following resource:

_____

_____

_____

_____

Rainer Maria Morita,

International Hidden Job Market Advisor

About the Author:

Rainer Maria Morita is an International Hidden Job Market Expert helping executives in Switzerland and worldwide find their perfect job based on his own job search methodology called the "Morita Method".

Each year, more than 1,000 executives profit from his expertise. Rainer Maria partners with top-tier executives and executive contenders worldwide to help them get an edge in this ever-changing international economy. He regularly coaches alumni from INSEAD and IMD. The largest outplacement company worldwide retains him for regular Hidden Job Market workshops covering Switzerland, Europe and Asia.

Rainer Maria is affiliated with Lausanne-based 50-strong consultancy Excelerate Partners. Rainer Maria is also an Executive Career Advisor with BlueSteps, headquartered in New York, which is the exclusive executive career service provider of the Association of Executive Search Consultants (AESC). AESC is the voice of excellence for the executive search and leadership consulting profession worldwide.

Rainer Maria is an international bestseller author who has published 7 books, notably "Executive Job Search in the Hidden Job Market – The Morita Method" and "Peak Performance Interviewing for Executives".

With a Masters in Strategic Technology and Innovation Management from the University of Manchester, UK, and Bocconi, Milan, combined with "AI Leadership" executive education at MIT, Boston, he is uniquely qualified to help leaders define how to best win in their transition towards the new normal.

Speaking Engagements:

Rainer is available internationally as a keynote speaker for speaking events. To ask Rainer to come and speak at your workplace, conference or industry association event, please contact: contact@HiddenExecutiveJobs.com

STAY IN TOUCH
FOLLOW ME AND CONTINUE TO BE INSPIRED

Follow me and continue to receive Support, Tools & Techniques, Encouragement, Pearls of Wisdom and Inspiration for your Career and Interview Success:

https://www.linkedin.com/in/rainerconnectyou/

https://www.instagram.com/rainermaria/

https://twitter.com/RainerMorita

https://www.facebook.com/rainer.morita

Hidden Job Market V-LOG

Register with my Hidden Job Market video blog. I am inspiring my blog readers with videos about remarkable leaders, gamechanging companies from different locations around the world:

To subscribe, click here:

https://www.youtube.com/channel/UCRZAOzsSkIgRSgAm-j4pODQ?view_as=subscriber

www.ingramcontent.com/pod-product-compliance
Lightning Source LLC
Chambersburg PA
CBHW050531210326
41520CB00012B/2527